the ocean

&

you

kiana azizian

there are only two things
in this world that i
have ever truly loved.

the ocean

&
then there's
you.

kiana azizian

the ocean

kiana azizian

i wasn't sure if
it would be possible,
growing compassionately,
blooming kind,
healing delicately.
it took strength and
courage i didn't know
i had within me.
but in the end,
the recipe was simple.
forgiveness,
with a bit of letting go.

not only forgiving others,
but the key was to forgive
myself for everything,
every time,
in every way.

this wind came
out of nowhere,
knocking us down,
messing us up,
tearing us apart.
then the rain.
it poured and poured.
flooded streets,
damaged homes,
broken hearts.
lives destroyed.
damage that cannot
be undone.

birds fled,
stars cried,
flowers died.
the world tossed
and then it turned.

as for you and i,

we'd never make
it back from this.

last night,
i prayed to the
sea to bring
you back to me.

- nightly prayer

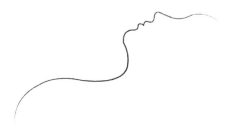

i am tired
of asking
the waves to
bring you back.

- prayer of the night

she's the type of storm you want to get lost in.

you told me
not to love you.
but i cannot
control the crashing
of the waves.

i'll hold on for you,
every night.
waiting,
watching the
sun go to sleep,
hoping maybe,
tomorrow,
with the day,
you'll come back
to me.

leave me to heal
on my own.

i never needed
you anyway.

i need someone who
will make me believe
in love again.

i need someone who
knows how to help me
come back together,
when i fall apart.

your memory
comes in waves.
and i am not sure,
i will survive
your storm tonight.

- i am drowning in your memories

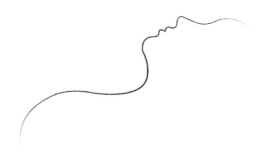

you should have taken
your memories with
you as you left.

- *i have no use for them anymore*

we all have that
one person we will
never really recover from.
that person,
who has carved
their names into our lungs.
expanding with every breath,
bleeding into our souls
with every moment,
every second.

and the key to healing
is accepting they will
forever be a part of us,
even if it hurts to utter
their name.

maybe they were right.
maybe i'm lost.
maybe i don't know who i am
or where i'm meant to be.
maybe i'm just a dreamer.
maybe i don't fit in.
in this society.
in this skin.
in this life.
maybe i'm too young.
maybe my life isn't
what it's supposed to be.
maybe my heart
isn't happy here.
maybe there's something
wrong with me.
maybe i'm just scared.
of failure.
of falling.
of you.
maybe i'm too much.

maybe i'm not enough.

you're a world away,
and i'm not sure how
to get to you.

- this distance is killing us

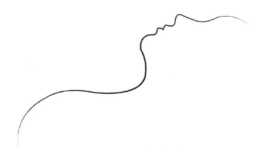

it will take me a lifetime to recover from you.

- how did you move on so quickly?

the waves tell our story.

the shore feels the weight
of us crashing down.

maybe you left because
you knew i deserved better.

maybe i let you because
i knew it too.

maybe we are just
better off
as two people
who can coexist
in this reckless world.

the sadness changes
and sometimes it fades.
but it never
does seem to truly leave.

oh my,
now it always
stays.

i can feel you,
gathering inside of me,
like the ocean.
carelessly,
wildly,
spreading into my veins.

i am part human,
part sea.
and without you,
i will drown away,
deeply,
into
nothing.

some days,
i want to change the world.

other days,
i want to disappear.

- there is no in-between

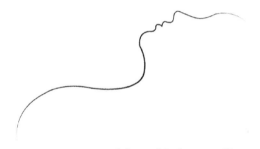

either this love will save us,
or destroy us.

there is no in-between.

- i'm still trying to decide which it will be

i'm not sure i'm in love with you anymore.

nine words i'll never recover from.

it seems
there is
no ocean
left for you
and me.

i still look for you
in the eyes of
every person i see.

after all this time,

how
   can
      this
         still
            be?

losing you was like losing air.

i could feel the life
unraveling from the
cavity of my lungs.

i am ready to live
outside the confinement
of your unrequited love.

i am ready to live
outside the prison
of your undeserving pain.

- release me

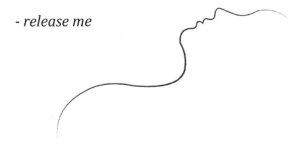

oh,
love and pain.

how well they go together.

- they cannot exist without each other

how much is enough,
before we lay this
thing to rest,
and let our hearts
get some sleep?

there's a fine line between
trying to please others
and following your heart.

- i hope you choose the latter.

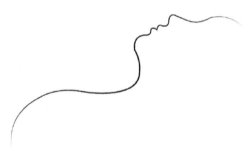

it is days like today
where i feel as if
these words
will get the
best of me.

- i've given everything to them

. . . but you are the only one my heart asks for.

it rained yesterday.
poured.

i broke with the sky.
falling apart,
tear by tear,
drop by drop,
until nothing
was left wading
inside of me.
except for all those
little stubborn
parts of you
that never seem
to fade away.

you were the lesson
my heart was too
stubborn to learn.

- persistent heart

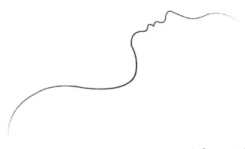

i do not know
how to live quietly,
calmly,
or cautiously.

- live loudly

have you
realized it yet?

how you'll
never find
another like me?

how no one
will ever
love you
with such
gentleness
as i once did?

how it will
always,
in the end,
come back
around
to me?

i am whole.

and that is something
you will never be able
to take away from me.

i'm drowning in a sea
of all the words i left unsaid.

- an ocean of regret

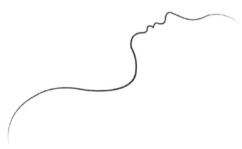

some days,
i like the rain.
how it washes the
thought of you away.

- rainy days

you come back to me
expecting me to open
my doors for you.
but i've changed the locks,
closed the windows,
drawn the blinds.
i've moved on.
moved forward.
and things are
different now.
i am different now.
i've redecorated,
remodeled,
renovated,
moved the furniture,
painted the walls red,
covered the place
in peonies.
no,
this is not your
home anymore.
no,
i am not your
home anymore.

and it's unfair to
expect me to be.

so i'll pretend this all
doesn't hurt so much,
and act as if the pain
has faded away.
i'll fantasize about not still
being in love with you,
until the day when i wake up
and it will be my truth.

it is the ocean that gives me hope.

i am giving my faith to the waves.

what if you and i
found our way back
to each other?

that would be
some kind
of magic.

15 Decembrie
2019

i wake each day and realize you
are no longer here.
and i crumble,
to ashes,
all over again.

- i am simply surviving without you

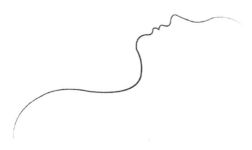

the birds flew away,
the trees cried,
the sky sulked,
the sun stayed in bed.

- none of us know what to do without you

even after all these years,
i am still trying to learn
how to make a home
out of this body.
how to fit into this skin,
and these bones.
i am still learning
how to grow,
bloom,
into myself.

why is it that they
always come back
when it's too late?

why is it that they
always come back
when we don't
need them?

why is it that they
always come back
when we have finally
found healing
within ourselves?

tonight,
i broke.
disappeared
into nothing.
but dust.
forgotten love,
neglected memories.

i am not sure
how i am
supposed to live,
when you are there,
i am here,
and there is everything,
yet nothing
between us?

the first time you touched me,
i turned into the sea:
soft,
wild,
enchantingly *free*.

- i am the sea in human form

i am aching to be
more than *just* the
girl you used to love.

- perhaps one day i will be

of all the things in
this world i cannot
understand,
why you left
is the only one that
still steals my
breath away.

i can still hear the
gentleness in your voice,
feel the tenderness
in your touch,
even with this ocean
that flows gently
between our shores.

- *even still*

there's got to be a
reason why we keep
running back to each other.
this thing between us
never really seems to fade.

- *maybe we weren't supposed to end like this*

just when i thought
i've escaped,
your grief finds me.
and even though
it has been years
since you've gone,
it remains,
unpacks.
it has become part of me.
it is as if your pain has
seeped into my blood
and convinced my
body it is my own.
persuaded me
i need it to live,
to function.
you linger and linger,
yet no part of you is
physically here.
you take and take,
but you never give.
you destroy,
devastate.

but you never heal.

once everything was
said and done,
i was left with nothing
but your old,
stained sweatshirt
and weeks of rain.

you stole the life from my lungs.

i am grateful for the strength that lives inside me.

never forget the person
you have become.

fight for yourself
every day.

i remember it all,
just like it was
only a few days ago.
how it felt in your arms,
hand in hand,
breath to breath,
watching the world go by,
laughing like we
knew all the answers
because we thought we did.
the smell of the sun
and the flowers,
drowning in the air.
a kiss for a kiss,
a touch for a touch.
we were in sync.
one as two.

two as one.

and when it feels like
the walls are caving in,
remember,
you are not alone in
this big messy world.
we are all in this together.
feeling,
thinking,
hurting in all
the same ways.
we are all just
yearning for something,
for someone,
to help us feel alive.
to help remind us we are living,
and that this life is not as
hard as we make it out to be.

how did it feel to know
that when you came
crawling back to me,
i didn't fall to my
knees for you?

i am reckless,
selfish.
i never say
the right things,
and when i do,
it's at the wrong time.
i am loud,
careless,
irresponsible.
i am messy.
and sometimes
i am even unkind.

but oh,
how i rage
like the sea.

how i am
courageously
free.

now,
getting lost in you
doesn't seem so
dangerous.

- i'm no longer scared of the fall

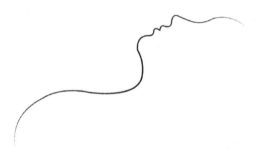

i'm a sucker for
bad guys
with wild eyes.

- they are my weakness

do you still feel me,
pulsing away,
in your veins?

do you still taste me
in your lungs?

even now,
after all this time,
i still linger,
remain.

have you ever
stopped and asked
yourself why that is?

you still linger,
lurk,
in the deepest,
darkest parts
of my heart.
even after all this time,
all these years,
you have become
a piece of me,
a part that i
never acknowledge,
but have accepted
as my own.
you never make
much noise,
quietly existing
in a space that has
now become ~~yours.~~
your home away from home.
and i know
that it's wrong.
but i am okay with this.
because at least
you are
still mine,
in some small,
subtle,
soft
kind of way. . .

i do what i can
to not think about you,
about the man who left,
the one who i wasn't good enough for.
i gave myself to you fully,
but you only gave
yourself in fragments.
little by little,
keeping me hooked,
addicted to the idea of actually being yours.
i stay awake at night,
thinking,
dreaming,
praying,
about you coming back to me.
the sound of your voice
telling me you missed me,
telling me you made a mistake,
that you were a fool.
you're such a fool.
but the fantasies fade,
and once again,
i am left with only small traces of you.
i close my eyes,
hoping i can replay
your memory again.
but the only thing
that comes is tears,

rain.

even though we
went our separate ways,
you will always
be with me.
you changed me,
forced me to become
a better version of myself.
you pushed me off the ledge
and forced me
to find my strength.
thanks to you,
i will never
question my worth again.
never doubt myself,
my abilities.
now that i know
what i am made of,
how resilient i am,
i am no longer
scared of my wings.
i am no longer
scared of the fall.

i am no longer
scared to fly.

the ocean still
makes me think of you.

how the wind
flowed through your hair,
the water gleamed,
blushed at you.
how easily the sand
caved at your touch,

and how the waves crashed,
disappeared,
as you ran away.

i was created by love,
yet it destroys me.
consumes me.
tears me apart
from the inside,
all the way to the out.

most days,
it feels as if i have
another world living,
raging,
inside of me,
pleading,
to be
set free.

there is this thunder that
still lives within you.
let that be a reminder
that you will always have
a little fight
left in those kind
bones of yours.

the sky weeps
and the sun bleeds
every time
you and your love leave.

- thunderstorms & darkness

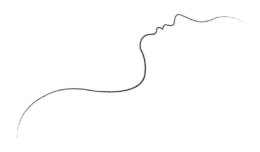

i cry with the rain,
scream with the wind,
fall with the sky.

- daughter of nature

it seems
like this world,
is nothing like what
my soul was anticipating.
this heaviness is
too much to bear.
this pain is
too much to endure.
i thought as i grew older,
i would find my place,
find my peace,
and that it would all
start to make
a little more sense.
but it seems that time
only creates more chaos.
answers lead to
more questions.
and those questions never
get answered.
the world keeps spinning,
and it doesn't
seem to ever slow down,
not for a moment,
not even for
one breath.

next time,
when you unravel
down to bone,
just know
there is still
hope in emptiness.

kiana azizian

i heard you've moved on,
met someone else.
and i'm not going to lie,
it hurt.

more than i thought it would.

but i know now that
this is the way
things are meant to be,
the way things are
supposed to be.
fate took you away.
then life led you
to someone else.

in the end,
all i can do is hope your
new life is peaceful.
that it gives you all
the things i didn't.

the things i couldn't give you.

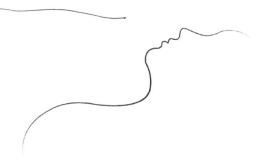

just because the
relationship is over
does not mean
the love has to end.

- true love never ends

things between us
were just simply,
complex.

- we didn't stand a chance

take your
heartbreak.
just leave.

you don't need
to worry
about me.

your touch is
heaven
in human form.

and i'm trying to
figure out how,
of all the people
on this earth,
you chose me to
hold in the palm
of your hand.

we're in too far,
too deep.

one of us isn't going
to make it out alive.

- i think it's me

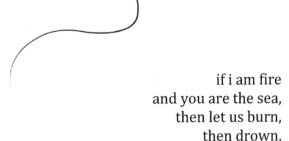

if i am fire
and you are the sea,
then let us burn,
then drown,
into one another.

- opposites attract

the day where i
don't recoil at the
thought of you
will become the
best day of my life.
it will become the day,
where i have finally
healed from your
destruction
and fallen in love
with my restoration.

i search for you
within the sky,
asking the stars
if they have
seen the man
who is out
of this world.

i was just a small
ripple in the ocean
of his love.
i'd drown before
he even noticed me.

it seems
i am no good at
this whole love thing,
this whole falling thing.
i fall too quickly,
forgive too easily,
and love too hard.

i fell to my knees
and surrendered
to the sea.
pleading to the waves
to forgive me.

please.

set me free.

ever since you broke me,
i've been looking
for healing,
peace,
in all the wrong people.

- i should be looking within

just when i think i've
gotten over you,
my mind asks
where it is you went,
and my heart weeps.

we all grieve.

and i think the world
feels it too.

her tears
turn into seawater.
her touch
blows the wind.
her sorrow
turns to thunder,
her pain
turns to lightning.

he should have known
i was a wild thing
(just like the sea),
he should have known
he couldn't hold me down.

if i could,
i would drown
in the ocean,
just to prove
how deep
my love is
for you.

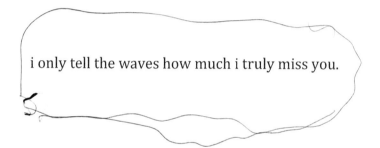

i only tell the waves how much i truly miss you.

kiana azizian

&
you

kiana azizian

i want to be
light like the
sun kissed morning,
free like the
waves of the sea,
soft like the
sound of your voice,
loved like
i am your everything.

you are gold.

and i'll never
stop treasuring you.

i will paint
you in my love.

this way,
you will
never be alone.

- i will always be here for you

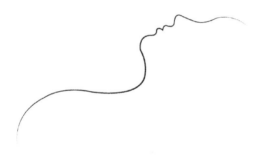

i hope you love with grace,
and fly with gratitude.

- let love be your wings

i'm too scared to
tell the sky about you,
because it would fall for you.
the sea would drown
at the thought of you.
the stars would burst
at your touch.
and the earth would
crumble to dust.

all just for you.

- i won't dare tell them, i promise

the ocean had a way
of calming her soul.
sun-kissed skin,
wavy hair,
and salty lips.

she lived for the sea,
because it had a way
of telling her story.
she found comfort
in its immensity,
somehow making her
feel a little less alone.

and as she sat,
watching the
waves kiss the shore,
she knew she'd
finally found a
place to call her own.
home.

you have a whole
another world
living inside of you.

how have you forgotten?

regret has never been
a word in my vocabulary.
there is no time to regret you.
you've already taken
more than you warrant.
thank you for coming,
loving,
and leaving.
i'm stronger now
than i've been before.
i am no longer mourning
the fragments of me
you took with you,
they are yours to keep.

all i have left for you now,
is forgiveness.

my heart falls for you,
day after day.
my skin unravels
at your touch.
my spine breaks
for your love.

i want to be yours,
continually,
always,
every single day,
in every single way.

set me on fire.

i want to burn for you.

- you are my fire

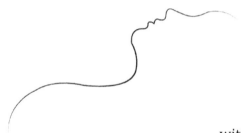

with you,
my heart
has turned
soft,

once again.

- and again

i'll wait for you
among the stars.

come find me
when you're ready.

you deserve someone
who sees past your scars
and searches for the
beauty within you.
you deserve love,
the real kind of love.
you deserve someone
who stays
and never even
considers walking away.

you,
my dear,
deserve the world.

and i hope,
one day,
you find your way.

step into your light.

it's time
to show the world
what you are
truly made of.

without you,
i am still me.
i am still whole,
worthy.
enough.
without you,
i am better,
kinder,
stronger.
without you,
i am finally given
the chance to
breathe on my own
and fall back in love
with the softness in
my soul.

take time growing
into yourself.
there is no rush,
my lovely.

in all the places
i find hope,
and in all the places
i find peace,
you
have always
been there.

you are in my blood,
in my veins,
and in my heart.

you are the pulse
that beats,
rages through me.

you are the one thing
that's keeping me alive.

there was just
something about
the way the
wind kissed you,
the sun blushed at you,
the world stopped for you.

i knew i needed
you in my life.

you can be
broken and beautiful
at the same time.

you do not have to
choose.

i hope you
find the strength
to believe in love again.
i hope you
find the type of
love you've
always deserved.
i hope you
find happiness.
in this life.
in love.
in yourself.
i hope you still
believe in magic,
in the little things.
i hope you still
believe in the
beauty of fate.
i hope you wake
every morning,
excited for what's
about to come.

i hope you find what
you were put on
this world to seek.
and once you do,
i hope that it is everything.

and even a little more.

her
~~his~~ kisses felt like coming home
after a lifetime of being lost.

- *finally*

you see,
my darling.
i have always been here,
waiting,
for you to come
back home to me.

- *always waiting*

you are the one
i have always
been hoping for.
stay,
please.
even if it's
just for a while.

i fell in love
with the kindness
in your eyes
and the gentleness
in your touch.

first,
you must
forgive yourself.
then everything
else will find a
way to work
itself out.

my fingertips kiss your skin
like you're my favorite story.
i want to read you over
and over.

- *then once again*

break into me.
forget all the love
you have lost.
surrender to the notion
of being mine
forever.

- *and i will be yours, always*

i am thankful for you.
your love.
your kindness.
your strength.
i am thankful for
your gentleness,
your forgiveness,
because it all helped me
find my way
back home
to myself.

i will love you until you see your light again.

it was your light that helped me find my way.

you are so full of light,
even the stars envy you.

- shine bright my dear

you talk to the wind;
i listen through the butterflies.

- natural conversations

it's the ones we don't see
coming that shake up our world,
putting us off track.
it's the ones we fall for slowly,
gradually,
gently.
one day at a time.
then suddenly,
we're not sure how
to exist without them.
it's the ones who aren't perfect,
yet still astonish us
with their imperfections.
it's the ones who never leave.
it's the ones who stay,
always.

i don't think i'll ever stop
falling
for
you.

- boundless love

my love is wild.
so fall,
recklessly into me.

- wild, wild love

you bring the trust.
i'll bring the love.
let's meet somewhere
in the middle,
my dear.

keep growing toward the sky.
the sun will welcome you home.

- coming home

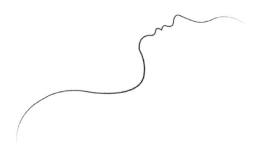

it's been so long.
welcome home.

we missed you.

- homecoming

i'm not entirely sure
what love is,
but i'm pretty sure it
looks something
like you.

this strength did
not come naturally.
i had to struggle,
battle,
endure until i finally found it.
only then did i realize
that just having
strength is not enough on its own.
i needed resilience,
perseverance,
so that i could keep
pushing through,
fighting back.
i needed kindness
in order to
keep my heart open,
in order to bloom.
mostly,
i needed to be soft,
so that i did not harden,
did not completely
lose my faith,
my humanity.

sunday mornings,
waking up in your arms,
sun shining on your face.
you slam the blinds shut,
blocking out any glimpse of light.
then you crawl back into bed,
pulling me closer,
bringing me into your chest,
while you rest your head on mine.
ten more minutes
you whisper in my ear.

i never want to wake up from this.

her

~~his~~ love has
made me humble,
kind,
soft,
human
once again.

her
- ~~his~~ love

her light is gentle,
soft,
kind.
let it bring out
the bright in you.

- *her light*

there's just
something about you;
you'll always have
a hold over me.

- *everlasting love*

forever,
with you,
is exactly where
i want to be.

- *you are my forever, my always.*

there's a sunrise in her skin,
a story in her destruction,
a strength in her pain,
a softness in her love.

this life is too short.

so,
come with me,
darling.
let's run away,
together.

i may not know
much about this life.
but one thing i do
know is that love,
will save us all.

- love is everything

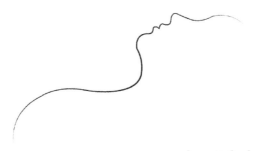

when it feels like
nothing is left,
there is always hope.

i can promise you that.

- you must have faith

i just hope
once you've found yourself,
you come back home to me.

i'll be waiting.

- always

i'm still waiting for you.

i'm always waiting for you.

- and i think i always will

this love,
our love,
is all that
you and i have.
so please,
darling,
linger a
little longer.
stay.

life is nothing but a
chaotic collection
of countless memories.

people come;
people go.

sometimes we fall in love;
other times we fall into pain.

but every time we slip,
we find our way back.

we are nothing but individuals,
trying to make our way,
find our place,
make our mark,
in this beautifully,
messy place,
we call home.

you kissed me
under the stars.
and for an instant,
it felt as if we
controlled the
entire universe.

she has a thing
for late nights,
sunsets in
unknown places,
with complete
strangers.

you came to me with
love dripping off your lips.

how did you expect me
to not fall madly for you?

- sugar lips

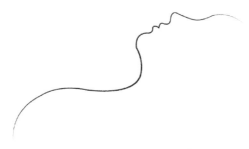

i see your love.
and all i want to do
is run
wildly into you.

-crash into me

in your moments
of hardship,
in your moments
of doubt,
uncertainty,
i will be there for you.

in your moments
of discovery,
bravery,
courage,
i will be rooting
for you.

i will always be
on your side.

because no matter
how hard we break,
how far we fall,
how bad we fail,
there is always a chance
at a new beginning,
a clean slate,
an opportunity to start over.
there is always redemption
waiting for us.
we are not defined
by the moments
that break us;
we are defined by the
courage it takes to
stand back up,
on our own.
we are made up
of the moment
we show the world
how far we have come.
and what kind of
magic we are made of.

i am hungry for love,
starving at the
thought of you,
collapsing at the notion
of you,
me,
us,
we,
together,
forever;

always.

fall tenderly,
slowly,
gently.

love hard,
passionately,
insanely.

live unapologetically,
daringly,
without any regrets.

kiana azizian

stop running back to
the people who broke you.
you will never find
peace in their broken arms.

she is wild,
free,
reckless.
she is a beautiful mess,
a gorgeous disaster.

i never knew to soften
would be so hard,
so difficult.
unlearning the pain,
remembering who we
were before it consumed
our lives,
our being,
before it ruined our innocence,
our purity.
no matter how hard we pushed,
we shoved,
we pulled,
the ache wouldn't fade.
it had become a part of us,
and we would never be the same.
this is when
we began to learn
how pain changes us.
we never really go
back to the person
we were before it.
we transform,
adapt,
grow,
and then we learn
to live with it all,
carrying it upon our souls,
weary of how it
will all end . . .

we made room for
this new version of ourselves,
grieving the parts
we have lost to this world.
the parts,
we have surrendered to this universe.
accepting that life has ended up
like nothing we
expected it to be,
like nothing we were promised
it was supposed to taste like.
so we try to find a new place
in this old world,
forgiving ourselves
for making mistakes
along the way.
you see,
the hurt doesn't ever leave.
it morphs into us
in ways we cannot understand,
let alone explain.
we fight,
too scared of letting go,
too scared of who we will become.
and in the end,
we just learn how to rise
and not let it consume
all of who we have somehow,
unexpectedly,
softened into.

release your guilt.

it is okay to put
yourself first;
honestly,
more than okay,
it is necessary.

your softness is just
as beautiful as you are,
my dear.

- your softness is stunning

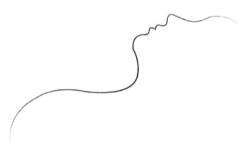

some days,
i am more ocean
than i am human.
i am more water
than i am fire.

- days like today

love should make you
be a better version
of yourself.

that's the
magic of it all.

that,
is what you
must look for.

when i pulled away,
you brought me closer
to your chest.
your heartbeat
is soothing,
it is kind.

it is calm,
like the sea.

i want to dive into you.
no hesitation.
no reservation.
no uncertainty.

just a little trust
and a lot of faith.

thank you for your love.

it was the
most beautiful
thing i have
and will ever know.

stay away from people
who constantly
try to change,
or complete you.
you are whole on your own.

- you do not need anyone else to be complete

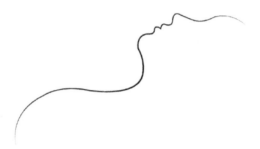

i have come too far
to let you calm the
storms within me.

- you will never stand in my way

at the end of the day,
the only thing that
remains in the darkness
of the night
is how kindly you love.

and how bravely you do so.

your journey
is beautiful.
the highs,
and the lows.
the lefts,
and the rights.
never be ashamed
of your path.
it has led you
to this place,
this space.
be proud of that.
be proud of how
much you have learned,
how far you've come,
and how far
you are about to grow.

do not accept
less than you deserve.
do not take
the easy way out.
do not choose
the lesser life.

please,
whatever you do,
never settle
for less than
you are worth.

i hope you
never feel stuck,
jammed into
a place where
you don't feel free.

even if it may
not feel like it,
it's okay to change.
yourself,
your mind,
your direction.
it's okay to suddenly
want different things
out of this life,
to see the world
in a different light.

this earth is
consistently rising,
changing.
we must grow
and transform
with the waves.

i think real
love is gentle,
it is kind
thoughtful
real love is tender,
just as much
as it is strong.

real love isn't
always perfect,
but it always tries.
it believes;
it has faith.

but most importantly,
true love never gives up.

love is messy,
unpredictable,
chaotic.
love is endless.
it is pure.
it is everything.
love brings joy,
but it also brings pain.
we must go through
the confusing parts,
to embrace the good.
love is forgiving.
sympathetic.
it makes mistakes,
does wrong.
it even disappoints.
but love is understanding.
it does not judge,
holds no grudges,
and carries no resentment.
love never gives up.
it's resilient,
strong.
it fights.
it battles.

it always remains.

loving yourself is about freedom:

freedom to breathe,
to be alive,
to be;
freedom to
follow your heart,
and see where it leads you.

please stay,
even if it hurts too much.
if your lungs give out,
and you hit rock bottom.

please stay,
even if i say
something reckless,
and you get angry.

please stay,
even if i make mistakes,
even if i drive you crazy.
even if i can't be enough.

please stay,
even if we scream,
if we fight
or shout.

please.
don't leave.

i hope whatever you do,
you always choose to
stay.

let love consume you,
use you,
and spit you back out.
let love overtake you,
overcome you.
let it be the reason
you get out of
bed in the morning,
the reason you are still here,
breathing,
beating,
thriving,
alive.
let love be
your everything,
and let it take
nothing from you,
not even yourself.
let love be your fire,
your spark,
ignition.
let love burn you up.
let it ruin you,
destroy you,
wreck you.
let love be
the end of you.

i'm not sure what
forever will bring us.

but for now,
we have this moment,
this breath,
and this love.

you see,
right now,
we have
everything we
will ever need.

there is light,
sincerity,
tenderness
in your eyes.

there is honesty,
freedom,
kindness
in your love.

come here.
embrace me.
close.
closer.
let us brave these
moonless nights.
and if we cannot
survive the dark
together,
let us love each
other until
we find our
light again.

i will be your light,
when you are suffocating
in the darkness of the night.

- i will be your lighthouse

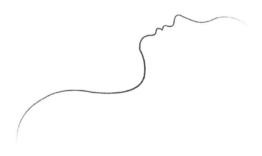

she carries the
stars in her eyes.
she is full of light.

- starry eyes

my light is
always on for you;
it shines
so that you can always
find your way,
back home to me.

— See me

→ To find me

Stand out

you,
are the breath
that brought
me back home
to myself
after years
of being lost.

look inside.
dig deep.
break open the parts
of you that you've shut
off for too long.
you've been through so much.
pain,
heartbreak,
loss,
and regret.
you've been hurt.
you've gotten your heart broken.
but you've also hurt others,
said things you probably
shouldn't have said,
and kept quiet when
words were what you needed.
you have made mistakes,
done yourself
and others wrong.
but you are just as human as they are.
the only thing left to do
is to forgive.
forgive yourself for it all.
this is the only way you
can move on and heal.
this is the only way to unravel,
and love yourself,
once again.

i just want you and me,
here,
now,
together,
forever.

- and always

as long as you
are by my side,
we can make it
through anything
together.

- together endlessly

i am ready to
break again.
to shatter,
smash,
collapse.
i am ready to
unravel,
undo.
i am ready to disengage,
to fall apart
without control,
direction,
without fear.

i am ready to
feel something real,
to feel something
far greater
than myself.

i think even
the ocean
would crumble
if it knew
how gentle
you really are.

your love
is my calm
in this messy
world of ours.

- messy peace

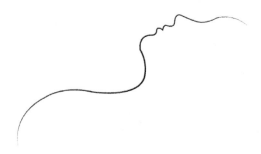

if i am not lost in your love,
i am lost in this world.

- i am lost without you

we are all struggling.
we are all hurting,
trying to heal.

yet we are all
too scared
to ask for help
and admit that
we are not okay
in this darkness.

- just know, that you are not alone

oh,
the way you love.

it even
brings the waves
to a halt,
calming,
guiding the sea,
shocking the sand.

i often wonder
about the person i was
before life left scars
all over my soul
and sorrow made
a home
out of my bones.

it's been so long.
it's time.

just let go.

- just be

so many of us need to
learn how to stand up
and put ourselves first,
pick ourselves up,
then walk away
when necessary.

change can be hard,
but change can
also be blissful.

these words are not for me.
they are for the girl who
cries herself to
sleep every night,
for the boy who never felt
like he was good enough,
manly enough.
these words are
for the dreamers,
the ones who believe
there is more out there
than this earth,
than this life.
the ones who never give up,
no matter how heavy life gets.
these words are for
the girl who starves herself
in order to feel like she can
fit into this world,
for the girl who has never
felt comfortable in
her own bones.

these words are for the
boy who could never
say the right thing,
never do the right things.
these words are for the
kindhearted people in this world.
the ones who give their all,
and never get enough in return.
these words are here to
remind you of
the softness of the world,
the kindness of the waves,
the gentleness of the universe.

eternally
&
always.

Printed by Amazon Italia Logistica S.r.l.
Torrazza Piemonte (TO), Italy

13140174R00099